THE
FINAL
MOMENTS

Critical Last-Day Events

SHAWN BOONSTRA

and Pacific Press Publishing Association

Contents

A Tale of Two Chapters

*Now I tell you before it comes,
that when it does come to pass,
you may believe that I am He.*
(John 13:19)

Sometimes, Christians make a tragic mistake when it comes to Bible prophecy. Instead of keeping ourselves busy with the work Christ assigned to the church—that of sharing the gospel with sinners—we hide ourselves away to work out the intricate details of how last-day events will play out. Armed with detailed charts and careful notes, we command quite a bit of attention in Bible study groups and prayer meetings—but at the same time, we couldn't tell you the names of our next door neighbors, because we haven't been praying for their salvation.

Is it important to understand last-day events? Absolutely. A good friend of mine used to say, "The future will not be kind to the uninformed," and I believe he was absolutely right. The time really has come for every believer to become reacquainted with the words of Daniel and Revelation, because in the near future, incredible changes are going to sweep our planet. "The final movements," said a very wise lady, "will be rapid ones." [1]

At the same time, however, the fulfillment of Bible prophecy ought to give us a new sense of urgency: there is work to be done. In Revelation 13, the Bible spells out the devil's end-time game plan in great detail, but it is only half of the prophetic picture. The other half is found in Revelation 14, where God's people are shown carrying His last message to every "nation, tribe, tongue, and people." (Revelation 14:6)

As we see the events described in Revelation 13 start playing out with greater speed and greater detail, we should recognize it as a call from God to *believe*. The work God has given His last-day movement will also play out with greater speed and in greater detail. The fulfillment of God's side of the controversy is just as certain as the devil's, and that means we cannot possibly fail in carrying out the commission that Jesus gave His church.

According to Christ, Bible prophecy is not so much about predicting the future as it is about recognizing the future when it happens. The fulfillment of prophecy vindicates our faith in Christ and gives us the courage we need to face the future. "I'm going to tell you these things now," Jesus told His disciples, "so that when they happen, you may believe that I am who I say I am."

Years ago, I used to live in the frozen north of the Alaska Highway. Sometimes, when the wind picked up in the winter, or the snowfall was unusually heavy at night, the road would almost completely disappear from view. It became impossible to tell where the edge of the highway ended and where the edge of the field began. I knew that if I were to veer off the road, I faced the distinct possibility of spending the night in my car, because I would be hopelessly trapped in the deep snow, and it was likely that nobody passing by would be able to see me. So I drove very carefully—my knuckles white from squeezing the steering wheel—constantly vigilant and incessantly praying that I'd be able to keep on the road.

And then I'd see it: a faint glow on the horizon, which told me I was almost home.

That's what Bible prophecy ought to do for us. In an increasingly dark and uncomfortable world, it ought to be the glow of home on the horizon. Far too many Christians live in sheer terror of the events portrayed in the book of Revelation because they only live in one chapter, Revelation 13. As we see the final details of that chapter unfolding, we ought to see them as a clear signal that God's Word is good—Revelation 14 is also unfolding. We are going to complete God's work successfully and make it home triumphantly.

A little while ago, a coworker put a little out-of-print booklet in my hand—which formed the basis for this book in your hand. That small booklet was *The Final Crisis and Deliverance,* which was compiled by Robert Odom and published by Southern Publishing Association many years ago.

As I thumbed through it, I discovered something re-markable: much of what Pastor Odom put in that booklet was still future to him. He didn't live to see it happen, and he would have had to imagine how the precise details of the prophecies would play out. Now we live in a time when we can actually see it taking shape.

Pastor Odom was a Seventh-day Adventist Christian. I myself did not grow up as a Seventh-day Adventist Christian. In my early twenties, I studied my way into this special movement of Christians with an open Bible. I found them to be a people who were deeply committed to Christ, had a remarkably vivid understanding of the gospel, and who adhered to a level of biblical fidelity I had never encountered before.

While much of the world has had to continually rework their understanding of Bible prophecy—reinterpreting key symbols every time the world's political situation shifts—Seventh-day Adventists have been amazingly consistent in their interpretation. That's because their broad-based, whole-Bible approach has made them somewhat impervious to the winds of change. With very few exceptions, they simply haven't had to change their minds on the details.

Additionally, they have also had access to a special collection of writings penned more than 100 years ago by a woman who had a remarkable gift and a deep connection with Christ. The Bible clearly predicts that in the last days, we should expect to find the Holy Spirit poured out on key individuals who will lead us into a deeper relationship with God.[2] Ellen White appears to have been blessed with that gift, and as a result, Seventh-day Adventists have come to treasure her writings.

In recent years, her work has been maligned by those who haven't actually read what she wrote. I have spent many hours reading her words, and have discovered that she exhibits an unusually high degree of biblical understanding. Her love for Jesus and His Word is unmistakable. While certainly not a substitute for the Bible, which stands alone as the supreme arbiter of the Christian faith, the words penned by Mrs. White so many decades ago ring truer now than they did when she first wrote them. In fact, the degree of accuracy she exhibits is breathtaking.

What you are about to read is a special collection of excerpts from her works which describe, in vivid detail, some of the events the Bible predicts will take place on our planet before Christ returns. This book assumes that the reader is well-acquainted with the book of Revelation and has studied it at some length.

We are living in very unusual times—the very times, it seems, described in the quotations you are about to read. It is our prayer that this book will serve as a catalyst to refuel your own passion for Christ and the work of His last-day movement of believers.

Shawn Boonstra
Speaker/Director
Voice of Prophecy
September 2015

---

1 *Testimonies for the Church, Vol. 9*, p. 11
2 See, for example, Joel 2:28

A THUMBNAIL SKETCH OF THE ISSUES
God's Claim on Our Worship

A careful reading of the book of Revelation reveals that the real issue in the last days has little to do with tanks and planes or political and economic disputes. The real issue is a matter of worship:

*And I saw one of his heads as if it had been mortally wounded, and his deadly wound was healed. And all the world marveled and followed the beast. So they **worshiped** the dragon who gave authority to the beast; and they worshiped the beast, saying, "Who is like the beast? Who is able to make war with him?" (Revelation 13:3, 4)*

*All who dwell on the earth will **worship** him, whose names have not been written in the Book of Life of the Lamb slain from the foundation of the world. (Revelation 13:8)*

*Then I saw another beast coming up out of the earth, and he had two horns like a lamb and spoke like a dragon. And he exercises all the authority of the first beast in his presence, and causes the earth and those who dwell in it to **worship** the first beast, whose deadly wound was healed. (Revelation 13:11, 12)*

*He was granted power to give breath to the image of the beast, that the image of the beast should both speak and cause as many as would not **worship** the image of the beast to be killed. (Revelation 13:15)*

A far more detailed biblical analysis of the key issues in Revelation 13 and 14 is available in *The Sign*. Visit vop.com/store to obtain a copy.

10

Before Christ returns, there will be a decisive call to the world for people to worship something—or someone—other than God. And in response, God's last-day people respond with a worldwide call to worship the Creator alone:

Then I saw another angel flying in the midst of heaven, having the everlasting gospel to preach to those who dwell on the earth—to every nation, tribe, tongue, and people—saying with a loud voice, "Fear God and give glory to Him, for the hour of His judgment has come; and **worship Him who made** *heaven and earth, the sea and springs of water." (Revelation 14:6, 7)*

In the final crisis, the real issues will revolve around worship and loyalty to the Creator. One side demands worship—forces it—under penalty of death; the other side pleads with the human race to return to Christ before it is too late.

Lucifer, once a covering cherub (an exalted position next to the throne of God; see Ezekiel 28:14), fell to his own pride and became dissatisfied with God's government. The Bible reveals that he began to covet the very throne of God and the worship that God receives from His creatures:

How you are fallen from heaven, O Lucifer, son of the morning! How you are cut down to the ground, you who weakened the nations! For you have said in your heart: "I will ascend into heaven, I will exalt my throne above the stars of God; I will also sit on the mount of the congregation on the farthest sides of the north; I will ascend above the heights of the clouds, I will be like the Most High." (Isaiah 14:12-14)

Again, the devil took Him up on an exceedingly high mountain, and showed Him all the kingdoms of the world and their glory. And he said to Him, "All these things I will give You if You will fall down and worship me." (Matthew 8:8, 9)

Let no one deceive you by any means; for that Day will not come unless the falling away comes first, and the man of sin is revealed, the son of perdition, who opposes and exalts himself above all that is called God or that is worshiped, so that he sits as God in the temple of God, showing himself that he is God. (2 Thessalonians 2:3, 4)

And I saw one of his heads as if it had been mortally wounded, and his deadly wound was healed. And all the world marveled and followed the beast. So they worshiped the dragon who gave authority to the beast; and they worshiped the beast, saying, "Who is like the beast? Who is able to make war with him?" (Revelation 13:3, 4)

So why, exactly, is Lucifer unworthy of worship? Other than his obvious defects in character, there is one underlying reason: he is not the Creator. All through Scripture, we find that God's claim to our worship is squarely based on His status as the One who made everything:

You alone are the Lord; you have made heaven, the heaven of heavens, with all their host, the earth and everything on it, the seas and all that is in them, and You preserve them all. The host of heaven worships You. (Nehemiah 9:6)

Thus you shall say to them: "The gods that have not made the heavens and the earth shall perish from the earth and from under these heavens." He has made the earth by His power, He has established the world by His wisdom, and has stretched out the heavens at His discretion. (Jeremiah 10:11, 12)

God, who made the world and everything in it, since He is Lord of heaven and earth, does not dwell in temples made with hands. Nor is He worshiped with men's hands, as though He needed anything, since He gives to all life, breath, and all things. (Acts 17:24, 25)

You are worthy, O Lord, to receive glory and honor and power; for You created all things, and by Your will they exist and were created. (Revelation 4:11)

Worship is clearly an important last-day issue. Another important thread that runs through Bible prophecy deals with **lawlessness.** Take a close look at some of Paul's predictions in other prophetic portions of the Bible:

Not everyone who says to Me, "Lord, Lord," shall enter the kingdom of heaven, but he who does the will of My Father in heaven. Many will say to Me in that day, "Lord, Lord, have we not prophesied in Your name, cast out demons in Your name, and done many wonders in Your name?" And then I will declare to them, "I never knew you; depart from Me, you who practice lawlessness!" (Matthew 7:21-23)

But know this, that in the last days perilous times will come: for men will be lovers of themselves, lovers of money, boasters, proud, blasphemers, disobedient to parents, unthankful, unholy, unloving, unforgiving, slanderers, without self-control, brutal, despisers of good, traitors, headstrong, haughty, lovers of pleasure rather than lovers of God, having a form of godliness but denying its power. And from such people turn away! (2 Timothy 3:1-5)

And then the lawless one will be revealed, whom the Lord will consume with the breath of His mouth and destroy with the brightness of His coming. The coming of the lawless one is according to the working of Satan, with all power, signs, and lying wonders... (2 Thessalonians 2:8, 9)

And the dragon was enraged with the woman, and he went to make war with the rest of her offspring, who keep the commandments of God and have the testimony of Jesus Christ. (Revelation 12:17)

Here is the patience of the saints; here are those who keep the commandments of God and the faith of Jesus. (Revelation 14:12)

That last verse—Revelation 14:12—is especially important, because it comes on the heels of a last-day warning to the world against worshiping the beast:

Then a third angel followed them, saying with a loud voice, "If anyone worships the beast and his image, and receives his mark on his forehead or on his hand, he himself shall also drink of the wine of the wrath of God, which is poured out full strength into the cup of His indignation." (Revelation 14:9, 10a)

The Bible reveals that the people of God "keep the commandments of God and the faith of Jesus." That would mean, of course, that those who worship the beast and receive his mark do *not* keep the commandments of God and have the faith of Jesus.

Piecing together all of the scriptural evidence, the key issues quickly rise to the surface. We've discovered that ***worship*** and ***lawlessness*** are primary issues. The devil wants to drive the world away from its Creator through deception and by forcing our worship in his direction. Those who resist the devil are clearly labeled as those who live in harmony with God's commandments and "worship Him who made." (Revelation 14:7) And amazingly, at the heart of God's moral law—His commandments—there is one requirement that outlines precisely how the Creator would like to be worshiped:

Remember the Sabbath day, to keep it holy. Six days you shall labor and do all your work, but the seventh day is the Sabbath of the Lord your God. In it you shall do no work: you, nor your son, nor your daughter, nor your male servant, nor your female servant, nor your cattle, nor your stranger who is within your gates. For in six days the Lord made the heavens and the earth, the sea, and all that is in them, and rested the seventh day. Therefore the Lord blessed the Sabbath day and hallowed it. (Exodus 20:8-11)

The language of the fourth commandment is strikingly similar to the final cry that goes to the earth in Revelation 14: "Worship Him who made heaven and earth, the sea and springs of water."

Furthermore, the Bible teaches that after God gave a copy of His moral law to the children of Israel, He asked them to write it in their hearts and minds:

And these words which I command you today shall be in your heart. You shall teach them diligently to your children, and shall talk of them when you sit in your house, when you walk by the way, when you lie down, and when you rise up. You shall bind them as a sign on your hand, and they shall be as frontlets between your eyes. (Deuteronomy 6:6-8)

Notice how God asked His people to "bind" His commandments on their hands and between their eyes —and also notice how the mark of the beast, which falls on those who worship wrongly under the devil's last-day counterfeit religion, is similarly located on the right hand or the forehead:

He was granted power to give breath to the image of the beast, that the image of the beast should both speak and cause as many

as would not worship the image of the beast to be killed. He causes all, both small and great, rich and poor, free and slave, to receive a mark on their right hand or on their foreheads.
(Revelation 13:15, 16)

Also notice that God's last-day people have the "Father's name" written on their foreheads:

Then I looked, and behold, a Lamb standing on Mount Zion, and with Him one hundred and forty-four thousand, having His Father's name written on their foreheads. (Revelation 14:1)

Is it a coincidence that God instructed Israel to write His commandments on their foreheads—and that God's last-day people have His name written in the same place? Absolutely not! To this day, we still speak of someone's "good name" when we refer to their good character. Jesus said that He had come to show the world God's "name." (John 17:6) The moral laws of God are not arbitrary rules—they are a clear revelation of God's perfect character. They show us His "name." When God says "thou shalt not steal," it demonstrates His honesty. When God says "thou shalt not kill," it demonstrates the value He places on life.

Popular interpretations of Bible prophecy would have us believe that the "mark of the beast" is a computer chip implanted in the hand or forehead, but the issues in Revelation are not that superficial. They have to do with loyalty and love. As events on planet Earth reach a climax, God will have a special people who have His name—His commandments—His character—written in their minds:

This is the covenant that I will make with them after those days, says the Lord: I will put My laws into their hearts, and in their minds I will write them. (Hebrews 10:16)

If you keep My commandments, you will abide in My love, just as I have kept My Father's commandments and abide in His love. (John 15:10)

If you love Me, keep My commandments. (John 14:15)

Interestingly, in modern Christianity, there is only one of God's Ten Commandments in dispute—the one dealing with the worship of the Creator. It is a sign of our relationship with God and our refusal to accept the devil's demands for worship:

Moreover I also gave them My Sabbaths, to be a sign between them and Me, that they might know that I am the Lord who sanctifies them. (Ezekiel 20:12)

I am the Lord your God: Walk in My statutes, keep My judgments, and do them; hallow My Sabbaths, and they will be a sign between Me and you, that you may know that I am the Lord your God. (Ezekiel 20:19, 20)

When you piece together all of the biblical evidence, it should come as no surprise to discover that the world has somehow forgotten the one commandment that begins with the word "remember"—the one requiring the seventh day of the week as a sign of loyalty to the God who made the heavens and the earth. Instead, most of the world now observes another day—the first day of the week—in spite of the fact that the Bible never gave the Christian church an instruction to change it.

It should also come as no surprise when we suddenly discover increasing demands to use the power of the state to enforce the observance of the first day of the week. In the 1880s, such a push started building in the United States. As I write these words, there is a continual push by the bishop of Rome for Sunday legislation. Whether this is simply one more wave in a long-term strategy to attempt to turn the world back toward Rome—or the beginning of the final events—remains to be seen.

Ultimately, the devil will demand that the world cast aside God's moral law and worship him instead.

Which day of the week you observe as the Sabbath may seem like a small issue to some, but it is not. Sunday is not the seventh day of the week. At Creation—and before sin (thus negating the argument that the Sabbath was established as part of the ceremonial or sacrificial system) —God set apart the seventh day as His own. He blessed it, rested on it, and sanctified it:

And on the seventh day God ended His work which He had done, and He rested on the seventh day from all His work which He had done. Then God blessed the seventh day and sanctified it, because in it He rested from all His work which God had created and made. (Genesis 2:2, 3)

Eating from the tree of the knowledge of good and evil seems like a small issue, too—but the point of abstaining was simply to demonstrate loyalty to God. The Sabbath gives us a unique opportunity, especially in the last days, to stand publicly against the devil's deceit and his demands for worship. It gives us an opportunity to publicly side with "Him who made."

What Donald Trump and the Pope Reveal About U.S. Politics

The two leaders have a surprising religious influence over the 2016 presidential race.

The U.S. political scene is interesting to say the least. Bigger-than-life personalities, mud-throwing, scandals, gaffes—there's never a dull moment. And of course, the whole process is permeated with more religion than almost any nation on Earth.

For all the talk about the secularization of the United States, it is still one of the most overtly Christian nations on Earth. (I'm talking profession, not behavior.) Professed atheists still struggle to get any traction on the political campaign trail. Last fall, an openly atheist candidate ran for Congress for the first time in U.S. history. One congressman (Pete Stark) admitted to being an atheist after he took office; he lost his 2012 re-election bid. Congressman Barney Frank announced he was gay back in 1987, but he waited until he left office to admit to being an atheist.

The so-called Moral Majority may not be the powerful lobby it once was, but Christianity continues to drive and shape public discussion and political debate in powerful ways, even though the U.S. Constitution is quite clear that "no religious test shall ever be required as a qualification to any public office."

The presumption of Christianity has obliged U.S. President Barack Obama to affirm his Christianity on more than one occasion. The same has been true for other presidents and presidential candidates.

Right now, 2016 presidential candidate Donald Trump appears to be positioning himself as a Christian candidate. Back in May, he announced that he would be "the greatest representative of the Christians they've had in a long time." He was referring to the plight of Syrian Christians, but his statement placed him on many evangelical voters' radars.

Trump, who identifies himself as a Presbyterian, also felt compelled to defend his Christianity when recently asked if he had ever asked God for forgiveness. His answer suggested a tragic lack of gospel understanding, but it was refreshingly honest—and it wasn't much different than many peoples' understanding of the gospel.

What was so refreshingly honest about it? Trump didn't pretend to be a "born-again" believer (in the sense that most U.S. evangelicals would understand the term) in order to win popularity. He could have started feeding the cameras what most Christians would want to hear, but he didn't. And the fact that he is openly friendly to Christianity seems, to some believers, to be good enough to crown him as a solid choice.

But Trump is not the only surprising religious influence in the coming race. A headline in the current issue of *TIME* magazine caught my attention: "Preaching Pope

Francis's Politics May Be the Key to Becoming President." The article wasn't entirely objective. It was actually a news commentary written by the executive director for Catholics in Alliance for the Common Good.

It was surprising nonetheless. Atheists are not the only ones who have struggled to gain traction in high-profile elections. Catholics have also struggled with acceptance over the years. As the article points out, back in 1960, John F. Kennedy had to assure the U.S. people that he wouldn't be taking orders from the pope in order to get elected.

If there was widespread suspicion about the Roman Catholic Church's influence on U.S. politics in the past, it seems to be all but over. On the list of current high-profile Catholic officeholders: the U.S. vice president, two-thirds of the U.S. Supreme Court justices, and the speaker of the U.S. House of Representatives.

Your great-grandparents would have been surprised. The wall of separation between church and state, enshrined in the Constitution, was erected to preserve religious liberty and keep the hands of the church off of anyone who didn't want the church touching them. It was a clear break with the power the Catholic Church had wielded for centuries in Europe. The constitutional separation wouldn't preclude Catholic candidates per se, but the desire to prevent the Catholic Church from gaining a political foothold in the United States was so powerful that the motives and loyalty of Catholic candidates were often doubted.

Fast-forward to the 2016 presidential race and the bishop of Rome has, ostensibly, become one of the most popular spokespersons in U.S.—and global—politics. Of course, becoming more popular than your average political candidate these days isn't all that impressive a feat, especially if you're not a political candidate, considering voter fatigue, immensely unpopular governments, and the way that U.S. politics has generally deteriorated over time. As opposed to many politicians, the pope's take-charge attitude and moral leadership seem refreshing to large numbers of people. He has become a powerful moral voice after a decades-long moral drought.

Pope Francis is scratching where many people are itching. He is a man of the disillusioned and the disenfranchised. He is challenging the global machinery of corporations and governments, and his audience is building. People disappointed with the world and its long string of political promise-breakers look to him as their next great hope. Upon his election in 2013, *TIME* magazine immediately crowned him Person of the Year. *Christianity Today* called him "our Francis, too," in an article explaining why the Christian world could now "enthusiastically join arms with the Catholic leader." His popular influence is hard to overestimate.

In late September 2015, Pope Francis will be addressing Congress, another first for U.S. government. In the words of *USA Today,* "No pope or religious leader who serves as a head of state has addressed Congress, according to the

U.S. House Historian's Office." Why? It's that church and state thing.

For students of U.S. government and history, the pope's influence is a surprising development. To students of Bible prophecy—well, they've been expecting things to begin trending this way for a long, long time.

The Final Crisis and Deliverance

Two great classes formed by the final test—the Sabbath

The Sabbath will be the great test of loyalty, for it is the point of truth especially controverted. When the final test shall be brought to bear upon men, then the line of distinction will be drawn between those who serve God and those who serve Him not. While the observance of the false sabbath in compliance with the law of the state, contrary to the fourth commandment, will be an avowal of allegiance to a power that is in opposition to God, the keeping of the true Sabbath, in obedience to God's law, is an evidence of loyalty to the Creator. While one class, by accepting the sign of submission to earthly powers, receive the mark of the beast, the other choosing the token of allegiance to divine authority, receive the seal of God.
The Great Controversy, p. 605

More light will come as the scroll unrolls

The light we have received upon the third angel's message is the true light. The mark of the beast is exactly what it has been proclaimed to be. Not all in regard to this matter is yet understood, nor will it be understood until

The Final Crisis and Deliverance, Robert Odom, editor.
Originally published by Southern Publishing Association.

the unrolling of the scroll; but a most solemn work is to be accomplished in our world.
Testimonies for the Church, Vol. 6, p. 17

People will unite under one head

As we approach the last crisis, it is of vital moment that harmony and unity exist among the Lord's instrumentalities. The world is filled with storm and war and variance. Yet under one head—the papal power—the people will unite to oppose God in the person of His witnesses.
Testimonies for the Church, Vol. 7, p. 182

What the mark of the beast is

The sign, or seal, of God is revealed in the observance of the seventh-day Sabbath, the Lord's memorial of creation. "The Lord spake unto Moses, saying, Speak thou also unto the children of Israel, saying, Verily My Sabbaths ye shall keep: for it is a sign between Me and you throughout your generations; that ye may know that I am the Lord that doth sanctify you." (Exodus 31:12, 13) Here the Sabbath is clearly designated as a sign between God and His people.

The mark of the beast is the opposite of this—the observance of the first day of the week. This mark distinguishes those who acknowledge the supremacy of the papal authority from those who acknowledge the authority of God. *Testimonies for the Church, Vol. 8*, p. 117

John was called to behold a people distinct from those who worship the beast or his image by keeping the first day of the week. The observance of this day is the mark of the beast. John declares, "Here is the patience of the saints: here are they that keep the commandments of God, and the faith of Jesus." *Testimonies to Ministers,* p. 133

The universal exaltation of Sunday will be the last act in the drama

The substitution of the false for the true is the last act in the drama. When this substitution becomes universal, God will reveal himself. When the laws of men are exalted above the laws of God, when the powers of this earth try to force men to keep the first day of the week, know that the time has come for God to work. He will arise in His majesty, and will shake terribly the earth. He will come out of His place to punish the inhabitants of the world for their iniquity. *Review and Herald,* April 23, 1901

The substitution of the laws of men for the law of God, the exaltation, by merely human authority, of Sunday in place of the Bible Sabbath, is the last act in the drama. When this substitution becomes universal, God will reveal Himself. He will arise in His majesty to shake terribly the earth. *Testimonies for the Church, Vol. 7,* p. 141

Protestantism will form a confederacy with the papacy

The professed Protestant world will form a confederacy with the man of sin, and the church and the world will be in corrupt harmony.

Here the great crisis is coming upon the world. The Scriptures teach that popery is to regain its lost supremacy, and that the fires of persecution will be rekindled through the time-serving concessions of the so-called Protestant world. *General Conference Daily Bulletin,* April 13, 1891

The Protestants of the United States will be the foremost actors

The Protestants of the United States will be foremost in stretching their hands across the gulf to grasp the hand of spiritualism; they will reach over the abyss to clasp hands with the Roman power; and under the influence of this threefold union, this country will follow in the steps of Rome in trampling on the rights of conscience.
The Great Controversy, p. 588

A National Sunday Law will be the act by which Protestants will join hands

When our nation shall so abjure the principles of its government as to enact a Sunday law, Protestantism will in this act join hands with popery; it will be nothing else than giving life to the tyranny which has long been eagerly watching its opportunity to spring again into active despotism. *Testimonies for the Church, Vol. 5,* p. 711

Protestantism is now forming the confederacy with popery

Protestantism is now reaching hands across the gulf to clasp hands with papacy, and a confederacy is being formed to trample out of sight the Sabbath of the fourth commandment; and the man of sin, who, at the instigation of Satan, instituted the spurious sabbath, this child of papacy, will be exalted to take the place of God.
An Appeal to Ministers and Conference Committees, p. 38

Protestant governments will participate

The Protestant governments will reach a strange pass. They will be converted to the world. They will also, in their separation from God, work to make falsehood and apostasy from God the law of the nation.

The General Conference Bulletin, January 1, 1900

How the image to the beast will be formed

In order for the United States to form an image of the beast, the religious power must so control the civil government that the authority of the state will also be employed by the church to accomplish her own ends.

The Great Controversy, p. 443

When the image of the beast will be formed

When the leading churches of the United States, uniting upon such points of doctrine as are held by them in common, shall influence the state to enforce their decrees and to sustain their institutions, then Protestant America will have formed an image of the Roman hierarchy, and the infliction of civil penalties upon dissenters will inevitably result. *The Great Controversy,* p. 445

What the image to the beast will be

The "image to the beast" represents that form of apostate Protestantism which will be developed when the Protestant churches shall seek the aid of the civil power for the enforcement of their dogmas. The "mark of the beast" still remains to be defined. *The Great Controversy,* p. 445

Only by changing God's law could the papacy exalt itself above God; whoever should understandingly keep the law as thus changed would be giving supreme honor to that power by which the change was made. Such an act of obedience to papal laws would be a mark of allegiance to the pope in the place of God. *The Great Controversy,* p. 446

How the worship of the beast and his image will be effected

The enforcement of Sunday-keeping on the part of Protestant churches is an enforcement of the worship of the papacy—of the beast. Those who, understanding the claims of the fourth commandment, choose to observe the false instead of the true Sabbath; are thereby paying homage to that power by which alone it is commanded. But in the very act of enforcing a religious duty by secular power, the churches would themselves form an image to the beast; hence the enforcement of Sunday-keeping in the United States would be an enforcement of the worship of the beast and his image.

The Great Controversy, p. 448 (1888)

When the mark of the beast will be received

Christians of past generations observed the Sunday, supposing that in so doing they were keeping the Bible Sabbath; and there are now true Christians in every church, not excepting the Roman Catholic communion, who honestly believe that Sunday is the Sabbath of divine appointment. God accepts their sincerity of purpose and their integrity before Him. But when Sunday observance shall be enforced by law, and the world shall be enlightened concerning the obligation of the true Sabbath, then whoever shall transgress the command of God, to obey a precept which has no higher authority than that of Rome, will thereby honor popery above God. He is paying homage to Rome and to the power which enforces the institution ordained by Rome. He is worshiping the beast and his image. As men then reject the institution which God has declared to be the sign of His authority, and honor in its stead that which Rome has chosen as the token of her supremacy, they will thereby accept the sign of allegiance to Rome—"the mark of the beast." And it is not until the issue is thus plainly set before the people, and they are brought to choose between the commandments of God and the commandments of men, that those who continue in transgression will receive "the mark of the beast."

The Great Controversy, p. 449

A Sunday law in free America

The dignitaries of church and state will unite to bribe, persuade, or compel all classes to honor the Sunday. The lack of divine authority will be supplied by oppressive enactments. Political corruption is destroying love of justice and regard for truth; and even in free America, rulers and legislators, in order to secure public favor, will yield to the popular demand for a law enforcing Sunday observance. Liberty of conscience, which has cost so great a sacrifice, will no longer be respected. In the soon-coming conflict we shall see exemplified the prophet's words: "The dragon was wroth with the woman, and went to make war with the remnant of her seed, which keep the commandments of God, and have the testimony of Jesus Christ." (Revelation 12:17) *The Great Controversy,* p. 592

National ruin will follow national apostasy

A time is coming when the law of God is, in a special sense, to be made void in our land. The rulers of our nation will, by legislative enactments, enforce the Sunday law, and thus God's people be brought into great peril. When our nation, in its legislative councils, shall enact laws to bind the consciences of men in regard to their religious privileges, enforcing Sunday observance, and bringing oppressive power to bear against those who keep the seventh-day Sabbath, the law of God will, to all intents and purposes, be made void in our land; and national apostasy will be followed by national ruin.

Review and Herald, December 18, 1888

It is at the time of the national apostasy, when, acting on the policy of Satan, the rulers of the land will rank themselves on the side of the man of sin—it is then the measure of guilt is full; the national apostasy is the signal for national ruin.

General Conference Daily Bulletin, April 13, 1891

The people of the United States have been a favored people; but when they restrict religious liberty, surrender Protestantism, and give countenance to popery, the measure of their guilt will be full, and "national apostasy"

will be registered in the books of heaven. The result of this apostasy will be national ruin.
Review and Herald, May 2, 1893

When our nation's cup will be full

By the decree enforcing the institution of the papacy in violation of the law of God, our nation will disconnect herself fully from righteousness. When Protestantism shall stretch her hand across the gulf to grasp the hand of the Roman power, when she shall reach over the abyss to clasp hands with spiritualism, when, under the influence of this threefold union, our country shall repudiate every principle of its Constitution as a Protestant and republican government, and shall make provision for the propagation of papal falsehoods and delusions, then we may know that the time has come for the marvelous working of Satan and that the end is near. *Testimonies for the Church, Vol. 5,* p. 451

This apostasy will be a sign that probation is about to close

As the approach of the Roman armies was a sign to the disciples of the impending destruction of Jerusalem, so may this apostasy be a sign to us that the limit of God's forbearance is reached, that the measure of our nation's iniquity is full, and that the angel of mercy is about to take her flight, never to return.
Testimonies for the Church, Vol. 5, p. 451

Loud cry sounded during storm of persecution

When the storm of persecution really breaks upon us, the true sheep will hear the true Shepherd's voice. Self-denying efforts will be put forth to save the lost, and many who have strayed from the fold will come back to follow the great Shepherd. The people of God will draw together and present to the enemy a united front. In view of the common peril, strife for supremacy will cease; there will be no disputing as to who shall be accounted greatest...

Thus will the truth be brought into practical life, and thus will be answered the prayer of Christ, uttered just before His humiliation and death: "That they all may be one; as Thou, Father, art in Me, and I in Thee, that they also may be one in Us: that the world may believe that Thou hast sent Me." (John 17:21) The love of Christ, the love of our brethren, will testify to the world that we have been with Jesus and learned of Him. Then will the message of the third angel swell to a loud cry, and the whole earth will be lightened with the glory of the Lord.
Testimonies for the Church, Vol. 6, p. 400

The Sabbath will be proclaimed more fully when trouble commences

At the commencement of the time of trouble, we were filled with the Holy Ghost as we went forth and proclaimed the Sabbath more fully. *Early Writings,* p. 33

"The commencement of that time of trouble," here mentioned does not refer to the time when the plagues shall begin to be poured out, but to a short period just before they are poured out, while Christ is in the sanctuary. At that time, while the work of salvation is closing, trouble will be coming on the earth, and the nations will be angry, yet held in check so as not to prevent the work of the third angel. At that time the "latter rain," or refreshing from the presence of the Lord, will come, to give power to the loud voice of the third angel, and prepare the saints to stand in the period when the seven last plagues shall be poured out. *Early Writings,* p. 85

The date of the close of probation has not been revealed

We are to bear the third angel's message to the world, warning men against the worship of the beast and his image, and directing them to take their places in the ranks of those who "keep the commandments of God, and have the faith of Jesus." God has not revealed to us the time when this message will close, or when probation will have an end. Those things that are revealed we shall accept for ourselves and for our children; but let us not seek to know that which has been kept secret in the councils of the Almighty. It is our duty to watch and work and wait, to labor every moment for the souls of men that are ready to perish. *Review and Herald,* October 9, 1894

A national Sunday law will be the signal for God's people to leave the large cities

As the siege of Jerusalem by the Roman armies was the signal for flight to the Judean Christians, so the assumption of power on the part of our nation in the decree enforcing the papal sabbath will be a warning to us. It will then be time to leave the large cities, preparatory to leaving the smaller ones for retired homes in secluded places among the mountains. *Testimonies for the Church, Vol. 5,* p. 464

Then shall be seen the dramatic working of Satan

Foreign nations will follow the example of the United States. Though she leads out, yet the same crisis will come upon our people in all parts of the world. *Testimonies for the Church, Vol. 6,* p. 395

As America, the land of religious liberty, shall unite with the papacy in forcing the conscience and compelling men to honor the false sabbath, the people of every country on the globe will be led to follow her example. Our people are not half awake to do all in their power, with the facilities within their reach, to extend the message of warning. *Testimonies for the Church, Vol. 6,* p. 18

In both the Old and the New World, the papacy will receive homage in the honor paid to the Sunday institution, that rests solely upon the authority of the Roman Church. *The Great Controversy,* p. 578 (see Matthew 24:24; 2 Thessalonians 2:9-12 and Revelation 13:13; 16:14)

When the cup of the nations will be full

God keeps a record with the nations: the figures are swelling against them in the books of heaven; and when it shall have become a law that the transgression of the first day of the week shall be met with punishment, then their cup will be full. *Review and Herald,* March 9, 1886

When the great crisis will come

This crisis will be reached when the nations shall unite in making void God's law.

Testimonies for the Church, Vol. 5, p. 523

This union will be seen as a grand move for the conversion of the world

Papists, Protestants, and worldlings will alike accept the form of godliness without the power, and they will see in this union a grand movement for the conversion of the world and the ushering in of the long-expected millennium. *The Great Controversy*, p. 588

Stricter Sunday observance will be demanded

It will be declared that men are offending God by the violation of the Sunday sabbath; that this sin has brought calamities which will not cease until Sunday observance shall be strictly enforced; and that those who present the claims of the fourth commandment, thus destroying reverence for Sunday, are troublers of the people, preventing their restoration to divine favor and temporal prosperity.

The Great Controversy, p. 590

Demons will second the testimony of religious leaders

The miracle-working power manifested through spiritualism will exert its influence against those who choose to obey God rather than men. Communications from the spirits will declare that God has sent them to convince the rejecters of Sunday of their error, affirming that the laws of the land should be obeyed as the law of God. They will lament the great wickedness in the world and second the testimony of religious teachers that the degraded state of morals is caused by the desecration of Sunday. Great will be the indignation excited against all who refuse to accept their testimony. *The Great Controversy,* p. 590

The faithful will be declared enemies of society

While Satan seeks to destroy those who honor God's law, he will cause them to be accused as lawbreakers, as men who are dishonoring God and bringing judgments upon the world. *The Great Controversy,* p. 591

Those who honor the Bible Sabbath will be denounced as enemies of law and order, as breaking down the moral restraints of society, causing anarchy and corruption, and calling down the judgments of God upon the earth. Their conscientious scruples will be pronounced obstinacy, stubbornness, and contempt of authority. They will be accused of disaffection toward the government. Ministers who deny the obligation of the divine law will present from the pulpit the duty of yielding obedience to the civil authorities as ordained of God. In legislative halls and courts of justice, commandment keepers will be misrepresented and condemned. A false coloring will be given to their words; the worst construction will be put upon their motives. *The Great Controversy,* p. 592

Calamities will be charged to God's people

I saw the sword, famine, pestilence, and great confusion in the land. The wicked thought that we had brought the judgments upon them, and they rose up and took counsel to rid the earth of us, thinking that then the evil would be stayed. *Early Writings,* p. 33

A death decree will be issued by the united powers of earth against God's people

The powers of earth, uniting to war against the commandments of God, will decree that "all, both small and great, rich and poor, free and bond" (Revelation 13:16), shall conform to the customs of the church by the observance of the false sabbath. All who refuse compliance will be visited with civil penalties, and it will finally be declared that they are deserving of death.
The Great Controversy, p. 604

It will be a universal death decree

Especially will the wrath of man be aroused against those who hallow the Sabbath of the fourth commandment; and at last a universal decree will denounce these as deserving of death. *Prophets and Kings,* p. 512

World leaders will consult together and issue the decree

I saw the saints leaving the cities and villages, and associating together in companies, and living in the most solitary places. Angels provided them food and water, while the wicked were suffering from hunger and thirst. Then I saw the leading men of the earth consulting together, and Satan and his angels busy around them. I saw a writing, copies of which were scattered in different parts of the land, giving orders that unless the saints should yield their peculiar faith, give up the Sabbath, and observe the first day of the week, the people were at liberty after a certain time to put them to death. But in this hour of trial the saints were calm and composed, trusting in God and leaning upon His promise that a way of escape would be made for them. In some places, before the time for the decree to be executed, the wicked rushed upon the saints to slay them; but angels in the form of men of war fought for them. Satan wished to have the privilege of destroying the saints of the Most High; but Jesus bade His angels watch over them. God would be honored by making a covenant with those who had kept His law, in the sight of the heathen round about them; and Jesus would be honored by translating, without their seeing death, the faithful, waiting ones who had so long expected Him. *Early Writings,* p. 282

What the death decree will demand

The decree will go forth that they must disregard the Sabbath of the fourth commandment, and honor the first day, or lose their lives.
Testimonies for the Church, Vol. 1, p. 353

A similar course will be pursued in both the old and the new world

As the Sabbath has become the special point of controversy throughout Christendom, and religious and secular authorities have combined to enforce the observance of the Sunday, the persistent refusal of a small minority to yield to the popular demand will make them

objects of universal execration. It will be urged that the few who stand in opposition to an institution of the church and a law of the state ought not to be tolerated; that it is better for them to suffer than for whole nations to be thrown into confusion and lawlessness... This argument will appear conclusive; and a decree will finally be issued against those who hallow the Sabbath of the fourth commandment, denouncing them as deserving of the severest punishment and giving the people liberty, after a certain time, to put them to death. Romanism in the Old World and apostate Protestantism in the New will pursue a similar course toward those who honor all the divine precepts.
The Great Controversy, p. 615

The death decree will be issued after the close of probation

I saw that the four angels would hold the four winds until Jesus' work was done in the sanctuary, and then will come the seven last plagues. These plagues enraged the wicked against the righteous; they thought that we had brought the judgments of God upon them, and that if they could rid the earth of us, the plagues would then be stayed. A decree went forth to slay the saints, which caused them to cry day and night for deliverance. This was the time of Jacob's trouble. *Early Writings,* p. 37

Then the time of Jacob's trouble for God's people will begin

The people of God will then be plunged into those scenes of affliction and distress described by the prophet as the time of Jacob's trouble. *The Great Controversy,* p. 616

The death decree will be similar to that issued by Ahasuerus

The decree which is to go forth against the people of God will be very similar to that issued by Ahasuerus against the Jews in the time of Esther.

Testimonies for the Church, Vol. 5, p. 450

A simultaneous move will be planned to kill God's people in one night

When the protection of human laws shall be withdrawn from those who honor the law of God, there will be, in different lands, a simultaneous movement for their destruction. As the time appointed in the decree draws near, the people will conspire to root out the hated sect. It will be determined to strike in one night a decisive blow, which shall utterly silence the voice of dissent and reproof.

The Great Controversy, p. 635

The death decree will be anticipated by some

Though a general decree has fixed the time when commandment keepers may be put to death, their enemies will in some cases anticipate the decree, and before the time specified, will endeavor to take their lives. But none can pass the mighty guardians stationed about every faithful soul. Some are assailed in their flight from the cities and villages; but the swords raised against them break and fall powerless as a straw. Others are defended by angels in the form of men of war. *The Great Controversy,* p. 631

God's people will be attacked at home and while in flight

In the time of trouble we all fled from the cities and

villages, but were pursued by the wicked, who entered the houses of the saints with a sword. They raised the sword to kill us, but it broke, and fell as powerless as a straw. *Early Writings,* p. 34

God would not suffer the wicked to destroy those who were expecting translation and who would not bow to the decree of the beast or receive his mark. I saw that if the wicked were permitted to slay the saints, Satan and all his evil host, and all who hate God, would be gratified. And oh, what a triumph it would be for his satanic majesty to have power, in the last closing struggle, over those who had so long waited to behold Him whom they loved! Those who have mocked at the idea of the saints' going up will witness the care of God for His people and behold their glorious deliverance.

As the saints left the cities and villages, they were pursued by the wicked, who sought to slay them. But the swords that were raised to kill God's people broke and fell as powerless as a straw. Angels of God shielded the saints. As they cried day and night for deliverance, their cry came up before the Lord. *Early Writings,* p. 284

Some of the faithful will be imprisoned

As the decree issued by the various rulers of Christendom against commandment keepers shall withdraw the protection of government and abandon them to those who desire their destruction, the people of God will flee from the cities and villages and associate together in companies, dwelling in the most desolate and solitary places. Many

will find refuge in the strongholds of the mountains. Like the Christians of the Piedmont valleys, they will make the high places of the earth their sanctuaries and will thank God for "the munitions of rocks." (Isaiah 33:16) But many of all nations and of all classes, high and low, rich and poor, black and white, will be cast into the most unjust and cruel bondage. The beloved of God pass weary days, bound in chains, shut in by prison bars, sentenced to be slain, some apparently left to die of starvation in dark and loathsome dungeons. No human ear is open to hear their moans; no human hand is ready to lend them help.
The Great Controversy, p. 626

Though enemies may thrust them into prison, yet dungeon walls cannot cut off the communication between their souls and Christ. One who sees their every weakness, who is acquainted with every trial, is above all earthly powers; and angels will come to them in lonely cells, bringing light and peace from heaven. The prison will be as a palace; for the rich in faith dwell there, and the gloomy walls will be lighted up with heavenly light as when Paul and Silas prayed and sang praises at midnight in the Philippian dungeon. *The Great Controversy,* p. 627

The wicked will be urged on by hosts of demons
Soon I saw the saints suffering great mental anguish. They seemed to be surrounded by the wicked inhabitants of the earth. Every appearance was against them. Some began to fear that God had at last left them to perish by the hand of the wicked. But if their eyes could have been

opened, they would have seen themselves surrounded by angels of God. Next came the multitude of the angry wicked, and next a mass of evil angels, hurrying on the wicked to slay the saints. But before they could approach God's people, the wicked must first pass this company of mighty, holy angels. This was impossible. The angels of God were causing them to recede and also causing the evil angels who were pressing around them to fall back.

It was an hour of fearful, terrible agony to the saints. Day and night they cried unto God for deliverance. To outward appearance, there was no possibility of their escape. The wicked had already begun to triumph, crying out, "Why doesn't your God deliver you out of our hands? Why don't you go up and save your lives?" But the saints heeded them not.

Like Jacob, they were wrestling with God. The angels longed to deliver them, but they must wait a little longer; the people of God must drink of the cup and be baptized with the baptism. The angels, faithful to their trust, continued their watch. God would not suffer His name to be reproached among the heathen. The time had nearly come when He was to manifest His mighty power and gloriously deliver His saints.
Early Writings, p. 283

The hour of deliverance

When the defiance of the law of Jehovah shall be almost universal, when His people shall be pressed in affliction by their fellow men, God will interpose. The fervent prayers of His people will be answered, for He

loves to have His people seek Him with all their heart, and depend upon Him as their Deliverer.
The General Conference Bulletin, January 1, 1900

The people of God—some in prison cells, some hidden in solitary retreats in the forests and the mountains—still plead for divine protection, while in every quarter companies of armed men, urged on by hosts of evil angels, are preparing for the work of death. It is now, in the hour of utmost extremity, that the God of Israel will interpose for the deliverance of His chosen.
The Great Controversy, p. 635

Deliverance will come at midnight

With shouts of triumph, jeering, and imprecation, throngs of evil men are about to rush upon their prey, when, lo, a dense blackness, deeper than the darkness of the night, falls upon the earth. Then a rainbow, shining with the glory from the throne of God, spans the heavens and seems to encircle each praying company. The angry multitudes are suddenly arrested. Their mocking cries die away. The objects of their murderous rage are forgotten. With fearful forebodings they gaze upon the symbol of God's covenant and long to be shielded from its overpowering brightness. *The Great Controversy,* p. 635

It is at midnight that God manifests His power for the deliverance of His people. The sun appears, shining in its strength. Signs and wonders follow in quick succession. The wicked look with terror and amazement upon the scene, while the righteous behold with solemn joy the tokens of their deliverance. Everything in nature seems turned out of its course. The streams cease to flow. Dark, heavy clouds come up and clash against each other. In the midst of the angry heavens is one clear space of indescribable glory, whence comes the voice of God like the sound of many waters, saying: "It is done." (Revelation 16:17)

That voice shakes the heavens and the earth. There is a mighty earthquake, "such as was not since men were upon the earth, so mighty an earthquake, and so great." (Revelation 16:17, 18) The firmament appears to open and shut. The glory from the throne of God seems flashing through. The mountains shake like a reed in the wind, and ragged rocks are scattered on every side. There is a roar as of a coming tempest. The sea is lashed into fury. There is heard the shriek of a hurricane like the voice of demons upon a mission of destruction. The whole earth heaves and swells like the waves of the sea. Its surface is breaking up. Its very foundations seem to be giving way. Mountain chains are sinking. Inhabited islands disappear. The seaports that have become like Sodom for wickedness are swallowed up by the angry waters. Babylon the great has come in remembrance before God, "to give unto her the cup of the wine of the fierceness of His wrath." Great hailstones, every one "about the weight of a talent," are doing their work of destruction. (Revelation 16:19, 21) The proudest cities of the earth are laid low. The lordly palaces, upon which the world's great men have lavished their wealth in order to glorify themselves, are crumbling to ruin before their eyes. Prison walls are rent asunder, and God's people, who have been held in bondage for their faith, are set free. *The Great Controversy,* p. 636

The wicked will slay each other with the arms intended to kill God's people

After the saints had been delivered by the voice of God, the wicked multitude turned their rage upon one another. The earth seemed to be deluged with blood, and dead bodies were from one end of it to the other. *Early Writings,* p. 289

The people see that they have been deluded. They accuse one another of having led them to destruction; but all unite in heaping their bitterest condemnation upon the ministers. Unfaithful pastors have prophesied smooth things; they have led their hearers to make void the law of God and to persecute those who would keep it holy. Now, in their despair, these teachers confess before the world their work of deception. The multitudes are filled with fury. "We are lost!" they cry, "and you are the cause of our ruin;" and they turn upon the false shepherds. The very ones that once admired them most will pronounce the most dreadful curses upon them. The very hands that once crowned them with laurels will be raised for their destruction. The swords which were to slay God's people are now employed to destroy their enemies. Everywhere there is strife and bloodshed. *The Great Controversy,* p. 655

The Deliverer comes

Soon there appears in the east a small black cloud, about half the size of a man's hand. It is the cloud which surrounds the Saviour and which seems in the distance to be shrouded in darkness. The people of God know this to be the sign of the Son of man. In solemn silence they gaze upon it as it draws nearer the earth, becoming lighter and more glorious, until it is a great white cloud, its base a glory like consuming fire, and above it the rainbow of the covenant. Jesus rides forth as a mighty conqueror.

The Great Controversy, p. 640